# JOBS IN THE NATIONAL GUARD

by Ashley Kuehl

Minneapolis, Minnesota

## Credits

Cover and title page, © The Washington Post /Getty Images and © Yoshinori Kuwahara/Getty Images; 5, © Sgt. Lianne Hirano/DVIDS; 7, © Master Sgt. Mike Smith/DVIDS; 9, © Spc. Adrianne Lopez/DVIDS; 11T, © Joseph Siemandel/DVIDS; 11B, © Staff Sgt. Heidi McClintock/DVIDS; 13T, © Petty Officer 1st Class Scott Bigley/DVIDS; 13B, © Senior Master Sgt. Beth Holliker/DVIDS; 15T, © Pfc. Arcadia Hammack/DVIDS; 15B, © Staff Sgt. Ronald Lafosse/DVIDS; 17, © Sgt. Richard Wrigley/DVIDS; 19T, © Master Sgt. Arthur Wright/DVIDS; 19B, © Master Sgt. Arthur Wright/DVIDS; 21, © Airman 1st Class Wynndermere Shaw/DVIDS; 23, © Staff Sgt. Emily Copeland/DVIDS; 25T, © Marcy Sanchez/DVIDS; 25B, © Staff Sgt. Leticia Samuels/DVIDS; 27, © Master Sgt. Becky Vanshur/DVIDS; 28T, © U. S. Army National Guard; 28B, © Henry Hudson Kitson/Wikimedia Commons; 29, © Minnesota National Guard/Wikimedia Commons, © SHARKY PHOTOGRAPHY/Adobe Stock, and © Dontstop/iStock.

**Bearport Publishing Company Product Development Team**
President: Jen Jenson; Director of Product Development: Spencer Brinker; Managing Editor: Allison Juda; Associate Editor: Naomi Reich; Associate Editor: Tiana Tran; Art Director: Colin O'Dea; Designer: Kim Jones; Designer: Kayla Eggert; Product Development Assistant: Owen Hamlin

**Statement on Usage of Generative Artificial Intelligence**
Bearport Publishing remains committed to publishing high-quality nonfiction books. Therefore, we restrict the use of generative AI to ensure accuracy of all text and visual components pertaining to a book's subject. See BearportPublishing.com for details.

Library of Congress Cataloging-in-Publication Data is available at www.loc.gov or upon request from the publisher.

ISBN: 979-8-89232-039-9 (hardcover)
ISBN: 979-8-89232-172-3 (ebook)

Copyright © 2025 Bearport Publishing Company. All rights reserved. No part of this publication may be reproduced in whole or in part, stored in any retrieval system, or transmitted in any form or by any means, electronic, mechanical, photocopying, recording, or otherwise, without written permission from the publisher. Bearport Publishing is a division of Chrysalis Education Group.

For more information, write to Bearport Publishing, 5357 Penn Avenue South, Minneapolis, MN 55419.

# CONTENTS

**Search and Rescue** ........................ 4
**The Oldest Fighting Force** ................ 6
**Joining the National Guard** ............... 10
**Weapons Jobs** ............................. 12
**Flying Safely** ............................ 14
**Maintaining Equipment** .................... 18
**Everything in Its Place** .................. 20
**Behind the Screens** ....................... 22
**Nurses and Physicians** .................... 24
**Taking Care of People** .................... 26

More about the National Guard .......... 28
Glossary.................................. 30
Read More................................. 31
Learn More Online......................... 31
Index..................................... 32
About the Author..........................32

# SEARCH AND RESCUE

A U.S. National Guard helicopter **hovers** above a city left flooded by a hurricane. Its pilots search for people stuck in the dangerously high water. They spot a group and lower the aircraft near the roof. A rescue team drops down to save the tired and injured from danger.

National guard helicopter pilots save people from disasters. They search for stranded people and drop off supplies to those in need. This is just one of the many important jobs in the United States National Guard.

### CAREER SPOTLIGHT: Helicopter Pilot

**Job Requirements:**
- At least 18 years old
- 9 to 24 weeks advanced training
- Officer

**Skills and Training:**
- Disaster Relief
- Security Operations
- Weather Navigation

National guard soldiers use rope to carry themselves up and down a helicopter.

# THE OLDEST FIGHTING FORCE

The United States National Guard is the oldest fighting force of the military. In fact, it began before the United States was even a country! In the early 1600s, a group of men worked together to protect the people and land of the 13 colonies. The Massachusetts Bay Colony sorted these fighters into **militia** groups. The groups fought against **Indigenous** peoples as well as Spanish and French colonizers.

This force has participated in all battles since then, fighting to defend the country and its people. However, it wasn't until 1915 that the military branch was officially named the national guard.

★ ★ ★ ★ ★ ★ ★ ★ ★

The militia groups also helped fight for the country's independence against Great Britain in the Revolutionary War (1775–1783).

Massachusetts Bay Colony militia

Today, the national guard is made up of two parts: the air and army national guard. The air guard is part of the U.S. Air Force, while the army guard is with the U.S. Army. Both parts are responsible for serving their community and country.

During peacetime, the national guard rescues people after disasters, such as wildfires or hurricanes. They also provide security for big community events. During wartime, the guard fights in battles all over the world.

Each U.S. state and territory has its own national guard. Its members usually protect their home states but they can be sent to help others, too.

National guard soldiers helped with security during Super Bowl LVIII.

# JOINING THE NATIONAL GUARD

Going through basic **combat** training is the first step to joining the national guard. These 10 weeks of training teach **recruits** about weapons, combat, and first aid. Most of training is spent building up their fitness. Recruits also practice facing the types of challenges they might see in action. They go through obstacle courses, climbing up and down towers, crawling on the ground, and more.

To graduate, recruits need to pass a fitness test made up of different challenges to prove their speed and strength. Once they've passed, recruits are officially national guard soldiers.

Most guard members work part-time. They are on duty for two weeks out of the year plus one weekend each month. But they may be called in whenever needed.

A national guard recruit pulling a weighted sled during a fitness test

# WEAPONS JOBS

Many military actions involve weapons. Explosive **ordnance** disposal specialists are experts in handling explosive weapons and materials. These soldiers work in the field, searching for hidden explosives during battle. Once explosives are found, the specialists decide the best ways to safely **defuse** them.

**Ammunition** specialists keep track of the weapon supplies, including the stock of guided missiles and rockets. They receive, store, and check weapons to see if any need to be repaired or replaced.

### CAREER SPOTLIGHT: Ammunition Specialist

**Job Requirements:**
- 17 to 35 years old
- 8 weeks and 2 days advanced training
- Enlisted

**Skills and Training:**
- Testing & Inspection
- Weapons Systems
- Explosives Operations

An explosive ordnance disposal specialist getting rid of an explosive

# FLYING SAFELY

Air traffic control operators are needed at military **bases**. These national guard soldiers tell pilots where to go and when it's safe to take off or land. The operators keep the many military aircraft from crashing into one another.

Weather and environmental science officers are experts in climate and weather conditions. They gather information about the wind, temperature, and clouds to predict the weather. This helps air teams plan the safest ways to get where they need to be.

### CAREER SPOTLIGHT: Air Traffic Control Operator

**Job Requirements:**
- 17 to 35 years old
- 17 weeks and 1 day advanced training
- Enlisted

**Skills and Training:**
- Communication
- Radar Operations
- Aircraft Procedures

**Uncrewed** aerial vehicle operators fly **drones** to gather information. These soldiers search for enemy locations and battle zones while controlling the drones from a distance. They may make maps, charts, and reports of what they find to send to soldiers on the ground nearby.

An RQ-7 operator flies **reconnaissance** drones to secretly collect information on enemy forces. The military can plan attacks based on what the operators learn.

### CAREER SPOTLIGHT: RQ-7 Operator

**Job Requirements:**
- At least 17 years old
- 15 weeks and 2 days advanced training
- Enlisted

**Skills and Training:**
- Piloting Uncrewed Aircraft
- Visual Analysis
- Surveillance & Detection

The RQ-7A Shadow 200 drone can take pictures and send them to ground forces.

# MAINTAINING EQUIPMENT

National guard members are needed to fix and maintain military equipment. A wheeled vehicle mechanic checks ground vehicles for damages, replacing and repairing broken parts as needed. Then, they test the vehicles to make sure the engines and systems are ready for their next mission.

Some guard soldiers take care of aircraft. An avionic mechanic provides maintenance for onboard communication and navigation systems. They look for any problems with the aircraft that could keep pilots from safely reaching their destinations.

### CAREER SPOTLIGHT: Wheeled Vehicle Mechanic

**Job Requirements:**
- 17 to 35 years old
- 14 weeks advanced training
- Enlisted

**Skills and Training:**
- Maintenance & Repairs
- Electronic Troubleshooting
- Electrical Systems

# EVERYTHING IN ITS PLACE

With thousands of soldiers working on different missions, keeping track of supplies and people is important. A transportation management coordinator makes sure that everything needed for a mission is where it needs to be. They plan and manage how and when gear and people get to where they're going all over the world.

An automated **logistical** specialist oversees equipment and supplies for a base. These specialists maintain supply records, making sure there is enough food, gear, and ammunition for missions.

### CAREER SPOTLIGHT: Automated Logistical Specialist

**Job Requirements:**
- 17 to 35 years old
- 9 weeks and 2 days advanced training
- Enlisted

**Skills and Training:**
- Record Keeping
- Data Analysis
- Stocking & Storage

# BEHIND THE SCREENS

Many national guard soldiers work together to keep information technology systems up and running. A **telecommunications** operator-maintainer protects communication networks from being attacked. Their job is to quickly respond to **cyber** threats, keeping an enemy from hacking into the military's communication systems.

Cyber operation officers protect communication and electronic systems, too. But they can also go on the offensive. Soldiers in this job may lead attacks on an enemy's cyber systems to gain knowledge about weapons or mission plans.

### CAREER SPOTLIGHT: Cyber Operations Officer

**Job Requirements:**
- Active duty
- 37 weeks officer training
- Officer

**Skills and Training:**
- Computer Systems & Networks
- Technical Procedures
- Cyber Operations

# NURSES AND PHYSICIANS

Like **civilians**, soldiers need help taking care of their health. A practical nursing specialist works with both soldiers and civilians. Sometimes, they are sent to the field to help soldiers hurt in battle. Other times, these specialists head to disaster areas to care for civilians in need.

Flight surgeons are trained **physicians** who work on moving aircraft, checking for illnesses and providing first aid to injured soldiers. They also help soldiers manage their physical and mental health.

### CAREER SPOTLIGHT: Practical Nursing Specialist

**Job Requirements:**
- At least 17 years old
- 51 weeks and 3 days advanced training
- Enlisted

**Skills and Training:**
- Emergency Medical Care
- Patient Care
- Chemistry & Biology

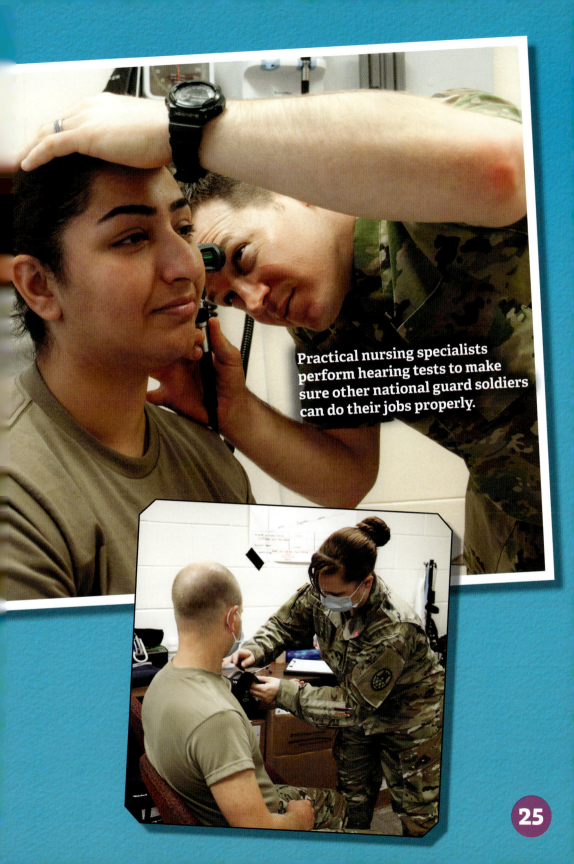

Practical nursing specialists perform hearing tests to make sure other national guard soldiers can do their jobs properly.

25

# TAKING CARE OF PEOPLE

Some jobs in the national guard are a lot like those in civilian life. **Chaplains** plan religious services. They help soldiers work through challenges in their lives. National guard band musicians provide music for ceremonies and entertainment.

From crews on the ground to those who take to the skies, the national guard is full of soldiers doing all kinds of jobs. Together, they help keep the national guard ready to protect the country and its people.

### CAREER SPOTLIGHT: Chaplain

**Job Requirements:**
- No less than 120 semester hours
- 12 weeks training
- Officer

**Skills and Training:**
- Religious Operations
- Workshops & Counseling
- Moral Support

# MORE ABOUT THE NATIONAL GUARD

## AT A GLANCE
**Founded:** December 13, 1636
**Membership:** Around 450,000
**Categories of ranks:** Enlisted soldier, officer, and warrant officer
**Largest base:** Camp Grayling in Grayling, Michigan

## DID YOU KNOW?

- The 54th Massachusetts Volunteer Infantry Regiment was one of the first Black American military units.

- During the Revolutionary War (1775–1783), some soldiers were called Minutemen. They were said to be ready to work at a minute's notice.

- Three presidents have served in the national guard: Theodore Roosevelt, Harry Truman, and George W. Bush.

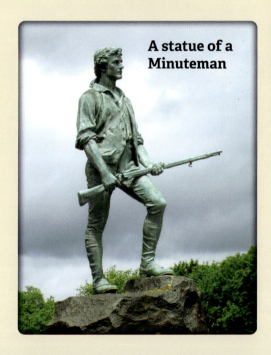

A statue of a Minuteman

# ★ GEAR ★

- WEAPON
- HELMET
- BACKPACK
- UNIFORM
- FOOD AND WATER
- BOOTS

29

# GLOSSARY

**ammunition** things that can be fired from weapons, such as bullets

**bases** places where the military keeps supplies or starts operations

**chaplains** religious leaders who work in the military, schools, or prisons

**civilians** people who are not in the armed forces or on a police force

**combat** fighting or having to do with fighting between soldiers or armies

**cyber** having to do with computers or computer networks

**defuse** to take apart a bomb to prevent it from exploding

**drones** aircraft without pilots that are operated remotely

**hovers** stays in one place in the air

**Indigenous** the original inhabitants of a place

**logistical** having to do with coordinating the details and parts of an operation or organization

**militia** a group of people who are trained to fight but are not professional soldiers

**ordnance** weapons and ammunition used by the military

**physicians** people with a medical degree who are trained and licensed to treat hurt and sick people

**reconnaissance** an exploration of enemy territory, with a goal of finding out information

**recruits** people who have recently joined the military

**telecommunications** the science of sending messages over long distances by radio, telephone, satellite, or other electronic systems

**uncrewed** not carrying people

# READ MORE

**Chandler, Matt.** *Drones (Torque: Military Science).* Minneapolis: Bellwether Media, 2022.

**Gagliardi, Sue.** *US National Guard (US Military).* Mendota Heights, MN: Apex Editions, 2023.

**Morey, Allan.** *U.S. National Guard (U.S. Armed Forces).* Minneapolis: Pogo Books, 2021.

# LEARN MORE ONLINE

1. Go to **www.factsurfer.com** or scan the QR code below.
2. Enter "**National Guard Jobs**" into the search box.
3. Click on the cover of this book to see a list of websites.

# INDEX

**aircraft** 4, 14, 16, 18, 24
**air traffic controllers** 14
**ammunitions** 12, 20
**basic combat training** 10
**chaplains** 26
**cyber** 22
**disasters** 4, 8, 24
**drones** 16–17
**explosives** 12–13
**fitness** 10–11
**helicopters** 4–5
**mechanics** 18
**missions** 18, 20, 22
**nurses** 24–25
**pilots** 4, 14, 16, 18
**physicians** 24
**Revolutionary War** 6, 28
**vehicles** 16, 18
**weapons** 10, 12, 22
**weather** 4, 14

# ABOUT THE AUTHOR

Ashley Kuehl is an editor and writer specializing in nonfiction for young people. She lives in Minneapolis, MN.